WHY DID HASHEM CREATE ME?

www.YechezkelStelzer.com

ISBN-10: 1-946351-69-5   ISBN-13: 978-1-946351-69-2

POSTCARD

Just like we can't give our children happiness, we can't give them self-esteem either. However, we can provide them with the building blocks, the love, and the care to help them develop it on their own.

Why Did Hashem Create Me? is one of those valuable building blocks that we can give children. This book provides a healthy perspective about G-d, life, and one-self that can strengthen a child's sense of worthiness and self-esteem and help them enjoy life more.

May you have much nachas from your children and see them grow up to be healthy and happy ovdei Hashem.

Rabbi Abraham J. Twerski, M.D.

Hashem made us all.
We know that, but why?
Some think
He was lonely in Heaven, up high.

1

But Hashem did not make us
for His **entertainment**,
Nor to boss us around.
That's **not** the arrangement.

He's not a tyrant who demands we obey,
To do certain things in exactly His way.

Hashem's not a super-being up in the sky,
Just looking and watching as the days go by.

Some people think that Hashem doesn't care,
That He forgot them, dislikes them,
or is simply not fair.

But Hashem isn't like that. In fact, you will find
That **Hashem** is infinitely loving and kind.

We can't fully grasp Him
with our human minds,
Because Hashem is completely
beyond space and time.

Hashem has created
each thing that exists,
From the galaxies and stars
to the knuckles on your fists.

8

So **why** did Hashem create you and **me**?

The truth is quite simple, as you will now see.

All Hashem wants is simply to give,
And that's why He gives us OUR lives to live.

That's why He made people, as an expression of love.
Every life, including yours, is a gift from above.

We have all been created to **live**, love, and play.
We were born to **enjoy** each and **every** day.

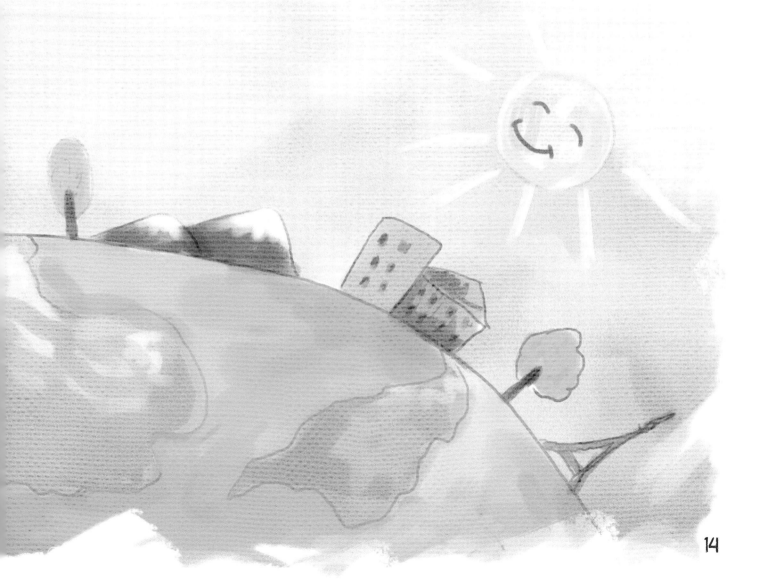

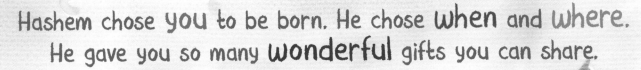

Hashem chose **you** to be born. He chose **when** and **where**.
He gave you so many **wonderful** gifts you can share.

Hashem created you to be just who you are,
Great and lovable! Made to shine, like a star!

But remember, your **greatness** is not a high score.
It's **not** about who can do better or **more**.

Your greatness is not about **whether** you win.
You will find your true greatness by **looking** within.

You have **goodness** inside you. Look and you'll see.
Be **happy** with who He made you to be.

19

When Hashem **breathed** your soul
into **your** body and mind,
He put **some** of His greatness
and wisdom **inside.**

Take a look at **yourself** and you will find,
You are **smart** and you're loving, joyful and **kind**.

Your soul is so pure, full of **goodness** and **light**.

Your soul is who you are – let it shine bright!

24

You have **something** to offer the **world**, all your own...

Something precious and special, that's yours alone.

No one walks just **your** path as they **live** out each day.
No one else sees the **world** in quite the same way.

There are so **many** things you are **able** to do!

And you do them so well just **because** you are you.

Don't worry if you make **mistakes** on the way.
Everyone does. It will all be okay.

Even when you don't **win**, even when you mess up...

You are never, **ever** unworthy of **love**.

Remember how truly amazing you are!
That's the most important thing by far.

There's **no doubt** about it – and don't say, "Yes, but..."
Hashem truly **loves** you, **no matter** what.

When you know you're a **gift** and that Hashem loves you,
There is no **light** brighter than the light that's in **you**.
Let it light up your life, and the **whole** world, too!